CW01192386

This daily chore book

Belongs to:

____

____

WEEKLY CHORE CHART

CHORES

	S	M	T	W	T	F	S

Notes

Reminders

WEEKLY CHORE CHART

CHORES	S	M	T	W	T	F	S

Notes

Reminders

WEEKLY CHORE CHART

CHORES	S	M	T	W	T	F	S

Notes

Reminders

WEEKLY CHORE CHART

CHORES	S	M	T	W	T	F	S

Notes

Reminders

WEEKLY CHORE CHART

CHORES	S	M	T	W	T	F	S

Notes

Reminders

WEEKLY CHORE CHART

CHORES	S	M	T	W	T	F	S
	☐	☐	☐	☐	☐	☐	☐
	☐	☐	☐	☐	☐	☐	☐
	☐	☐	☐	☐	☐	☐	☐
	☐	☐	☐	☐	☐	☐	☐
	☐	☐	☐	☐	☐	☐	☐
	☐	☐	☐	☐	☐	☐	☐
	☐	☐	☐	☐	☐	☐	☐
	☐	☐	☐	☐	☐	☐	☐
	☐	☐	☐	☐	☐	☐	☐

Notes

Reminders

WEEKLY CHORE CHART

CHORES	S	M	T	W	T	F	S
	☐	☐	☐	☐	☐	☐	☐
	☐	☐	☐	☐	☐	☐	☐
	☐	☐	☐	☐	☐	☐	☐
	☐	☐	☐	☐	☐	☐	☐
	☐	☐	☐	☐	☐	☐	☐
	☐	☐	☐	☐	☐	☐	☐
	☐	☐	☐	☐	☐	☐	☐
	☐	☐	☐	☐	☐	☐	☐
	☐	☐	☐	☐	☐	☐	☐

Notes

Reminders

WEEKLY CHORE CHART

CHORES

	S	M	T	W	T	F	S

Notes

Reminders

WEEKLY CHORE CHART

CHORES	S	M	T	W	T	F	S
	☐	☐	☐	☐	☐	☐	☐
	☐	☐	☐	☐	☐	☐	☐
	☐	☐	☐	☐	☐	☐	☐
	☐	☐	☐	☐	☐	☐	☐
	☐	☐	☐	☐	☐	☐	☐
	☐	☐	☐	☐	☐	☐	☐
	☐	☐	☐	☐	☐	☐	☐
	☐	☐	☐	☐	☐	☐	☐
	☐	☐	☐	☐	☐	☐	☐

Notes

Reminders

WEEKLY CHORE CHART

CHORES	S	M	T	W	T	F	S
	☐	☐	☐	☐	☐	☐	☐
	☐	☐	☐	☐	☐	☐	☐
	☐	☐	☐	☐	☐	☐	☐
	☐	☐	☐	☐	☐	☐	☐
	☐	☐	☐	☐	☐	☐	☐
	☐	☐	☐	☐	☐	☐	☐
	☐	☐	☐	☐	☐	☐	☐
	☐	☐	☐	☐	☐	☐	☐
	☐	☐	☐	☐	☐	☐	☐

Notes

Reminders

WEEKLY CHORE CHART

CHORES	S	M	T	W	T	F	S

Notes

Reminders

WEEKLY CHORE CHART

CHORES	S	M	T	W	T	F	S

Notes

Reminders

WEEKLY CHORE CHART

CHORES	S	M	T	W	T	F	S

Notes

Reminders

WEEKLY CHORE CHART

CHORES	S	M	T	W	T	F	S
	☐	☐	☐	☐	☐	☐	☐
	☐	☐	☐	☐	☐	☐	☐
	☐	☐	☐	☐	☐	☐	☐
	☐	☐	☐	☐	☐	☐	☐
	☐	☐	☐	☐	☐	☐	☐
	☐	☐	☐	☐	☐	☐	☐
	☐	☐	☐	☐	☐	☐	☐
	☐	☐	☐	☐	☐	☐	☐
	☐	☐	☐	☐	☐	☐	☐

Notes

Reminders

WEEKLY CHORE CHART

CHORES	S	M	T	W	T	F	S
	☐	☐	☐	☐	☐	☐	☐
	☐	☐	☐	☐	☐	☐	☐
	☐	☐	☐	☐	☐	☐	☐
	☐	☐	☐	☐	☐	☐	☐
	☐	☐	☐	☐	☐	☐	☐
	☐	☐	☐	☐	☐	☐	☐
	☐	☐	☐	☐	☐	☐	☐
	☐	☐	☐	☐	☐	☐	☐
	☐	☐	☐	☐	☐	☐	☐

Notes

Reminders

WEEKLY CHORE CHART

CHORES	S	M	T	W	T	F	S

Notes

Reminders

WEEKLY CHORE CHART

CHORES	S	M	T	W	T	F	S

Notes

Reminders

WEEKLY CHORE CHART

CHORES

Chores	S	M	T	W	T	F	S
	☐	☐	☐	☐	☐	☐	☐
	☐	☐	☐	☐	☐	☐	☐
	☐	☐	☐	☐	☐	☐	☐
	☐	☐	☐	☐	☐	☐	☐
	☐	☐	☐	☐	☐	☐	☐
	☐	☐	☐	☐	☐	☐	☐
	☐	☐	☐	☐	☐	☐	☐
	☐	☐	☐	☐	☐	☐	☐
	☐	☐	☐	☐	☐	☐	☐

Notes

Reminders

WEEKLY CHORE CHART

CHORES

	S	M	T	W	T	F	S

Notes

Reminders

WEEKLY CHORE CHART

CHORES	S	M	T	W	T	F	S
	☐	☐	☐	☐	☐	☐	☐
	☐	☐	☐	☐	☐	☐	☐
	☐	☐	☐	☐	☐	☐	☐
	☐	☐	☐	☐	☐	☐	☐
	☐	☐	☐	☐	☐	☐	☐
	☐	☐	☐	☐	☐	☐	☐
	☐	☐	☐	☐	☐	☐	☐
	☐	☐	☐	☐	☐	☐	☐
	☐	☐	☐	☐	☐	☐	☐

Notes

Reminders

WEEKLY CHORE CHART

CHORES

	S	M	T	W	T	F	S

Notes

Reminders

WEEKLY CHORE CHART

CHORES

S	M	T	W	T	F	S

Notes

Reminders

WEEKLY CHORE CHART

CHORES

S	M	T	W	T	F	S
☐	☐	☐	☐	☐	☐	☐
☐	☐	☐	☐	☐	☐	☐
☐	☐	☐	☐	☐	☐	☐
☐	☐	☐	☐	☐	☐	☐
☐	☐	☐	☐	☐	☐	☐
☐	☐	☐	☐	☐	☐	☐
☐	☐	☐	☐	☐	☐	☐
☐	☐	☐	☐	☐	☐	☐
☐	☐	☐	☐	☐	☐	☐

Notes

Reminders

WEEKLY CHORE CHART

CHORES	S	M	T	W	T	F	S
	☐	☐	☐	☐	☐	☐	☐
	☐	☐	☐	☐	☐	☐	☐
	☐	☐	☐	☐	☐	☐	☐
	☐	☐	☐	☐	☐	☐	☐
	☐	☐	☐	☐	☐	☐	☐
	☐	☐	☐	☐	☐	☐	☐
	☐	☐	☐	☐	☐	☐	☐
	☐	☐	☐	☐	☐	☐	☐
	☐	☐	☐	☐	☐	☐	☐

Notes

Reminders

WEEKLY CHORE CHART

CHORES

	S	M	T	W	T	F	S

Notes

Reminders

WEEKLY CHORE CHART

CHORES	S	M	T	W	T	F	S

Notes

Reminders

WEEKLY CHORE CHART

CHORES

S M T W T F S

Notes

Reminders

WEEKLY CHORE CHART

CHORES

S	M	T	W	T	F	S

Notes

Reminders

WEEKLY CHORE CHART

CHORES

	S	M	T	W	T	F	S
	☐	☐	☐	☐	☐	☐	☐
	☐	☐	☐	☐	☐	☐	☐
	☐	☐	☐	☐	☐	☐	☐
	☐	☐	☐	☐	☐	☐	☐
	☐	☐	☐	☐	☐	☐	☐
	☐	☐	☐	☐	☐	☐	☐
	☐	☐	☐	☐	☐	☐	☐
	☐	☐	☐	☐	☐	☐	☐
	☐	☐	☐	☐	☐	☐	☐

Notes

Reminders

WEEKLY CHORE CHART

CHORES	S	M	T	W	T	F	S

Notes

Reminders

WEEKLY CHORE CHART

CHORES

CHORES	S	M	T	W	T	F	S

Notes

Reminders

WEEKLY CHORE CHART

CHORES	S	M	T	W	T	F	S

Notes

Reminders

WEEKLY CHORE CHART

CHORES	S	M	T	W	T	F	S

Notes

Reminders

WEEKLY CHORE CHART

CHORES	S	M	T	W	T	F	S
	☐	☐	☐	☐	☐	☐	☐
	☐	☐	☐	☐	☐	☐	☐
	☐	☐	☐	☐	☐	☐	☐
	☐	☐	☐	☐	☐	☐	☐
	☐	☐	☐	☐	☐	☐	☐
	☐	☐	☐	☐	☐	☐	☐
	☐	☐	☐	☐	☐	☐	☐
	☐	☐	☐	☐	☐	☐	☐
	☐	☐	☐	☐	☐	☐	☐

Notes

Reminders

WEEKLY CHORE CHART

CHORES

	S	M	T	W	T	F	S
	☐	☐	☐	☐	☐	☐	☐
	☐	☐	☐	☐	☐	☐	☐
	☐	☐	☐	☐	☐	☐	☐
	☐	☐	☐	☐	☐	☐	☐
	☐	☐	☐	☐	☐	☐	☐
	☐	☐	☐	☐	☐	☐	☐
	☐	☐	☐	☐	☐	☐	☐
	☐	☐	☐	☐	☐	☐	☐
	☐	☐	☐	☐	☐	☐	☐

Notes

Reminders

WEEKLY CHORE CHART

CHORES	S	M	T	W	T	F	S
	☐	☐	☐	☐	☐	☐	☐
	☐	☐	☐	☐	☐	☐	☐
	☐	☐	☐	☐	☐	☐	☐
	☐	☐	☐	☐	☐	☐	☐
	☐	☐	☐	☐	☐	☐	☐
	☐	☐	☐	☐	☐	☐	☐
	☐	☐	☐	☐	☐	☐	☐
	☐	☐	☐	☐	☐	☐	☐
	☐	☐	☐	☐	☐	☐	☐

Notes

Reminders

WEEKLY CHORE CHART

CHORES	S	M	T	W	T	F	S

Notes

Reminders

WEEKLY CHORE CHART

CHORES	S	M	T	W	T	F	S

Notes

Reminders

WEEKLY CHORE CHART

CHORES

S	M	T	W	T	F	S

Notes

Reminders

WEEKLY CHORE CHART

CHORES

	S	M	T	W	T	F	S

Notes

Reminders

WEEKLY CHORE CHART

CHORES	S	M	T	W	T	F	S

Notes

Reminders

WEEKLY CHORE CHART

CHORES

	S	M	T	W	T	F	S
	☐	☐	☐	☐	☐	☐	☐
	☐	☐	☐	☐	☐	☐	☐
	☐	☐	☐	☐	☐	☐	☐
	☐	☐	☐	☐	☐	☐	☐
	☐	☐	☐	☐	☐	☐	☐
	☐	☐	☐	☐	☐	☐	☐
	☐	☐	☐	☐	☐	☐	☐
	☐	☐	☐	☐	☐	☐	☐
	☐	☐	☐	☐	☐	☐	☐

Notes

Reminders

WEEKLY CHORE CHART

CHORES

S	M	T	W	T	F	S

Notes

Reminders

WEEKLY CHORE CHART

CHORES	S	M	T	W	T	F	S

Notes

Reminders

WEEKLY CHORE CHART

CHORES	S	M	T	W	T	F	S

Notes

Reminders

WEEKLY CHORE CHART

CHORES

	S	M	T	W	T	F	S

Notes

Reminders

WEEKLY CHORE CHART

CHORES

CHORES	S	M	T	W	T	F	S

Notes

Reminders

WEEKLY CHORE CHART

CHORES	S	M	T	W	T	F	S

Notes

Reminders

WEEKLY CHORE CHART

CHORES

	S	M	T	W	T	F	S

Notes

Reminders

WEEKLY CHORE CHART

CHORES

	S	M	T	W	T	F	S

Notes

Reminders

WEEKLY CHORE CHART

CHORES

	S	M	T	W	T	F	S
	☐	☐	☐	☐	☐	☐	☐
	☐	☐	☐	☐	☐	☐	☐
	☐	☐	☐	☐	☐	☐	☐
	☐	☐	☐	☐	☐	☐	☐
	☐	☐	☐	☐	☐	☐	☐
	☐	☐	☐	☐	☐	☐	☐
	☐	☐	☐	☐	☐	☐	☐
	☐	☐	☐	☐	☐	☐	☐
	☐	☐	☐	☐	☐	☐	☐

Notes

Reminders

WEEKLY CHORE CHART

CHORES	S	M	T	W	T	F	S
	☐	☐	☐	☐	☐	☐	☐
	☐	☐	☐	☐	☐	☐	☐
	☐	☐	☐	☐	☐	☐	☐
	☐	☐	☐	☐	☐	☐	☐
	☐	☐	☐	☐	☐	☐	☐
	☐	☐	☐	☐	☐	☐	☐
	☐	☐	☐	☐	☐	☐	☐
	☐	☐	☐	☐	☐	☐	☐
	☐	☐	☐	☐	☐	☐	☐

Notes

Reminders

WEEKLY CHORE CHART

CHORES

CHORES	S	M	T	W	T	F	S

Notes

Reminders

WEEKLY CHORE CHART

CHORES

Chores	S	M	T	W	T	F	S

Notes

Reminders

WEEKLY CHORE CHART

CHORES

	S	M	T	W	T	F	S
	☐	☐	☐	☐	☐	☐	☐
	☐	☐	☐	☐	☐	☐	☐
	☐	☐	☐	☐	☐	☐	☐
	☐	☐	☐	☐	☐	☐	☐
	☐	☐	☐	☐	☐	☐	☐
	☐	☐	☐	☐	☐	☐	☐
	☐	☐	☐	☐	☐	☐	☐
	☐	☐	☐	☐	☐	☐	☐
	☐	☐	☐	☐	☐	☐	☐

Notes

Reminders

WEEKLY CHORE CHART

CHORES	S	M	T	W	T	F	S

Notes

Reminders

WEEKLY CHORE CHART

CHORES

	S	M	T	W	T	F	S

Notes

Reminders

WEEKLY CHORE CHART

CHORES	S	M	T	W	T	F	S

Notes

Reminders

WEEKLY CHORE CHART

CHORES

S	M	T	W	T	F	S

Notes

Reminders

WEEKLY CHORE CHART

CHORES	S	M	T	W	T	F	S

Notes

Reminders

WEEKLY CHORE CHART

CHORES	S	M	T	W	T	F	S

Notes

Reminders

WEEKLY CHORE CHART

CHORES

	S	M	T	W	T	F	S

Notes

Reminders

WEEKLY CHORE CHART

CHORES	S	M	T	W	T	F	S

Notes

Reminders

WEEKLY CHORE CHART

CHORES	S	M	T	W	T	F	S
	☐	☐	☐	☐	☐	☐	☐
	☐	☐	☐	☐	☐	☐	☐
	☐	☐	☐	☐	☐	☐	☐
	☐	☐	☐	☐	☐	☐	☐
	☐	☐	☐	☐	☐	☐	☐
	☐	☐	☐	☐	☐	☐	☐
	☐	☐	☐	☐	☐	☐	☐
	☐	☐	☐	☐	☐	☐	☐
	☐	☐	☐	☐	☐	☐	☐

Notes

Reminders

WEEKLY CHORE CHART

CHORES	S	M	T	W	T	F	S

Notes

Reminders

WEEKLY CHORE CHART

CHORES

	S	M	T	W	T	F	S
	☐	☐	☐	☐	☐	☐	☐
	☐	☐	☐	☐	☐	☐	☐
	☐	☐	☐	☐	☐	☐	☐
	☐	☐	☐	☐	☐	☐	☐
	☐	☐	☐	☐	☐	☐	☐
	☐	☐	☐	☐	☐	☐	☐
	☐	☐	☐	☐	☐	☐	☐
	☐	☐	☐	☐	☐	☐	☐
	☐	☐	☐	☐	☐	☐	☐

Notes

Reminders

WEEKLY CHORE CHART

CHORES

	S	M	T	W	T	F	S

Notes

Reminders

WEEKLY CHORE CHART

CHORES

	S	M	T	W	T	F	S

Notes

Reminders

WEEKLY CHORE CHART

CHORES

	S	M	T	W	T	F	S

Notes

Reminders

WEEKLY CHORE CHART

CHORES	S	M	T	W	T	F	S

Notes

Reminders

WEEKLY CHORE CHART

CHORES

	S	M	T	W	T	F	S
	☐	☐	☐	☐	☐	☐	☐
	☐	☐	☐	☐	☐	☐	☐
	☐	☐	☐	☐	☐	☐	☐
	☐	☐	☐	☐	☐	☐	☐
	☐	☐	☐	☐	☐	☐	☐
	☐	☐	☐	☐	☐	☐	☐
	☐	☐	☐	☐	☐	☐	☐
	☐	☐	☐	☐	☐	☐	☐
	☐	☐	☐	☐	☐	☐	☐

Notes

Reminders

WEEKLY CHORE CHART

CHORES

S	M	T	W	T	F	S

Notes

Reminders

WEEKLY CHORE CHART

CHORES

	S	M	T	W	T	F	S

Notes

Reminders

WEEKLY CHORE CHART

CHORES	S	M	T	W	T	F	S
	☐	☐	☐	☐	☐	☐	☐
	☐	☐	☐	☐	☐	☐	☐
	☐	☐	☐	☐	☐	☐	☐
	☐	☐	☐	☐	☐	☐	☐
	☐	☐	☐	☐	☐	☐	☐
	☐	☐	☐	☐	☐	☐	☐
	☐	☐	☐	☐	☐	☐	☐
	☐	☐	☐	☐	☐	☐	☐
	☐	☐	☐	☐	☐	☐	☐

Notes

Reminders

WEEKLY CHORE CHART

CHORES

	S	M	T	W	T	F	S

Notes

Reminders

WEEKLY CHORE CHART

CHORES

	S	M	T	W	T	F	S

Notes

Reminders

WEEKLY CHORE CHART

CHORES	S	M	T	W	T	F	S
	☐	☐	☐	☐	☐	☐	☐
	☐	☐	☐	☐	☐	☐	☐
	☐	☐	☐	☐	☐	☐	☐
	☐	☐	☐	☐	☐	☐	☐
	☐	☐	☐	☐	☐	☐	☐
	☐	☐	☐	☐	☐	☐	☐
	☐	☐	☐	☐	☐	☐	☐
	☐	☐	☐	☐	☐	☐	☐
	☐	☐	☐	☐	☐	☐	☐

Notes

Reminders

WEEKLY CHORE CHART

CHORES

	S	M	T	W	T	F	S

Notes

Reminders

WEEKLY CHORE CHART

CHORES

S	M	T	W	T	F	S

Notes

Reminders

WEEKLY CHORE CHART

CHORES

	S	M	T	W	T	F	S

Notes

Reminders

WEEKLY CHORE CHART

CHORES

	S	M	T	W	T	F	S
	☐	☐	☐	☐	☐	☐	☐
	☐	☐	☐	☐	☐	☐	☐
	☐	☐	☐	☐	☐	☐	☐
	☐	☐	☐	☐	☐	☐	☐
	☐	☐	☐	☐	☐	☐	☐
	☐	☐	☐	☐	☐	☐	☐
	☐	☐	☐	☐	☐	☐	☐
	☐	☐	☐	☐	☐	☐	☐
	☐	☐	☐	☐	☐	☐	☐

Notes

Reminders

WEEKLY CHORE CHART

CHORES	S	M	T	W	T	F	S

Notes

Reminders

WEEKLY CHORE CHART

CHORES	S	M	T	W	T	F	S

Notes

Reminders

WEEKLY CHORE CHART

CHORES	S	M	T	W	T	F	S

Notes

Reminders

WEEKLY CHORE CHART

CHORES

S	M	T	W	T	F	S

Notes

Reminders

WEEKLY CHORE CHART

CHORES

	S	M	T	W	T	F	S

Notes

Reminders

WEEKLY CHORE CHART

CHORES	S	M	T	W	T	F	S

Notes

Reminders

WEEKLY CHORE CHART

CHORES	S	M	T	W	T	F	S

Notes

Reminders

WEEKLY CHORE CHART

CHORES	S	M	T	W	T	F	S

Notes

Reminders

WEEKLY CHORE CHART

CHORES

	S	M	T	W	T	F	S
	☐	☐	☐	☐	☐	☐	☐
	☐	☐	☐	☐	☐	☐	☐
	☐	☐	☐	☐	☐	☐	☐
	☐	☐	☐	☐	☐	☐	☐
	☐	☐	☐	☐	☐	☐	☐
	☐	☐	☐	☐	☐	☐	☐
	☐	☐	☐	☐	☐	☐	☐
	☐	☐	☐	☐	☐	☐	☐
	☐	☐	☐	☐	☐	☐	☐

Notes

Reminders

WEEKLY CHORE CHART

CHORES

	S	M	T	W	T	F	S

Notes

Reminders

WEEKLY CHORE CHART

CHORES	S	M	T	W	T	F	S

Notes

Reminders

WEEKLY CHORE CHART

CHORES

CHORES	S	M	T	W	T	F	S

Notes

Reminders

WEEKLY CHORE CHART

CHORES	S	M	T	W	T	F	S

Notes

Reminders

WEEKLY CHORE CHART

CHORES	S	M	T	W	T	F	S
	☐	☐	☐	☐	☐	☐	☐
	☐	☐	☐	☐	☐	☐	☐
	☐	☐	☐	☐	☐	☐	☐
	☐	☐	☐	☐	☐	☐	☐
	☐	☐	☐	☐	☐	☐	☐
	☐	☐	☐	☐	☐	☐	☐
	☐	☐	☐	☐	☐	☐	☐
	☐	☐	☐	☐	☐	☐	☐
	☐	☐	☐	☐	☐	☐	☐

Notes

Reminders

WEEKLY CHORE CHART

CHORES	S	M	T	W	T	F	S

Notes

Reminders

WEEKLY CHORE CHART

CHORES

S	M	T	W	T	F	S
☐	☐	☐	☐	☐	☐	☐
☐	☐	☐	☐	☐	☐	☐
☐	☐	☐	☐	☐	☐	☐
☐	☐	☐	☐	☐	☐	☐
☐	☐	☐	☐	☐	☐	☐
☐	☐	☐	☐	☐	☐	☐
☐	☐	☐	☐	☐	☐	☐
☐	☐	☐	☐	☐	☐	☐
☐	☐	☐	☐	☐	☐	☐

Notes

Reminders

WEEKLY CHORE CHART

CHORES

S	M	T	W	T	F	S
☐	☐	☐	☐	☐	☐	☐
☐	☐	☐	☐	☐	☐	☐
☐	☐	☐	☐	☐	☐	☐
☐	☐	☐	☐	☐	☐	☐
☐	☐	☐	☐	☐	☐	☐
☐	☐	☐	☐	☐	☐	☐
☐	☐	☐	☐	☐	☐	☐
☐	☐	☐	☐	☐	☐	☐
☐	☐	☐	☐	☐	☐	☐

Notes

Reminders

WEEKLY CHORE CHART

CHORES

S	M	T	W	T	F	S

Notes

Reminders

WEEKLY CHORE CHART

CHORES

S	M	T	W	T	F	S

Notes

Reminders

WEEKLY CHORE CHART

CHORES	S	M	T	W	T	F	S

Notes

Reminders

WEEKLY CHORE CHART

CHORES

	S	M	T	W	T	F	S
	☐	☐	☐	☐	☐	☐	☐
	☐	☐	☐	☐	☐	☐	☐
	☐	☐	☐	☐	☐	☐	☐
	☐	☐	☐	☐	☐	☐	☐
	☐	☐	☐	☐	☐	☐	☐
	☐	☐	☐	☐	☐	☐	☐
	☐	☐	☐	☐	☐	☐	☐
	☐	☐	☐	☐	☐	☐	☐
	☐	☐	☐	☐	☐	☐	☐

Notes

Reminders

WEEKLY CHORE CHART

CHORES

S	M	T	W	T	F	S

Notes

Reminders

WEEKLY CHORE CHART

CHORES	S	M	T	W	T	F	S

Notes

Reminders

WEEKLY CHORE CHART

CHORES

S	M	T	W	T	F	S

Notes

Reminders

WEEKLY CHORE CHART

CHORES	S	M	T	W	T	F	S
	☐	☐	☐	☐	☐	☐	☐
	☐	☐	☐	☐	☐	☐	☐
	☐	☐	☐	☐	☐	☐	☐
	☐	☐	☐	☐	☐	☐	☐
	☐	☐	☐	☐	☐	☐	☐
	☐	☐	☐	☐	☐	☐	☐
	☐	☐	☐	☐	☐	☐	☐
	☐	☐	☐	☐	☐	☐	☐
	☐	☐	☐	☐	☐	☐	☐

Notes

Reminders

WEEKLY CHORE CHART

CHORES

S	M	T	W	T	F	S

Notes

Reminders

WEEKLY CHORE CHART

CHORES

	S	M	T	W	T	F	S
	☐	☐	☐	☐	☐	☐	☐
	☐	☐	☐	☐	☐	☐	☐
	☐	☐	☐	☐	☐	☐	☐
	☐	☐	☐	☐	☐	☐	☐
	☐	☐	☐	☐	☐	☐	☐
	☐	☐	☐	☐	☐	☐	☐
	☐	☐	☐	☐	☐	☐	☐
	☐	☐	☐	☐	☐	☐	☐
	☐	☐	☐	☐	☐	☐	☐

Notes

Reminders

WEEKLY CHORE CHART

CHORES

	S	M	T	W	T	F	S

Notes

Reminders

WEEKLY CHORE CHART

CHORES	S	M	T	W	T	F	S

Notes

Reminders

WEEKLY CHORE CHART

CHORES	S	M	T	W	T	F	S

Notes

Reminders

WEEKLY CHORE CHART

CHORES	S	M	T	W	T	F	S
	☐	☐	☐	☐	☐	☐	☐
	☐	☐	☐	☐	☐	☐	☐
	☐	☐	☐	☐	☐	☐	☐
	☐	☐	☐	☐	☐	☐	☐
	☐	☐	☐	☐	☐	☐	☐
	☐	☐	☐	☐	☐	☐	☐
	☐	☐	☐	☐	☐	☐	☐
	☐	☐	☐	☐	☐	☐	☐
	☐	☐	☐	☐	☐	☐	☐

Notes

Reminders

WEEKLY CHORE CHART

CHORES	S	M	T	W	T	F	S

Notes

Reminders

WEEKLY CHORE CHART

CHORES

S M T W T F S

Notes

Reminders

WEEKLY CHORE CHART

CHORES

	S	M	T	W	T	F	S

Notes

Reminders

WEEKLY CHORE CHART

CHORES	S	M	T	W	T	F	S

Notes

Reminders

WEEKLY CHORE CHART

CHORES

S	M	T	W	T	F	S

Notes

Reminders

WEEKLY CHORE CHART

CHORES	S	M	T	W	T	F	S
	☐	☐	☐	☐	☐	☐	☐
	☐	☐	☐	☐	☐	☐	☐
	☐	☐	☐	☐	☐	☐	☐
	☐	☐	☐	☐	☐	☐	☐
	☐	☐	☐	☐	☐	☐	☐
	☐	☐	☐	☐	☐	☐	☐
	☐	☐	☐	☐	☐	☐	☐
	☐	☐	☐	☐	☐	☐	☐
	☐	☐	☐	☐	☐	☐	☐

Notes

Reminders

WEEKLY CHORE CHART

CHORES	S	M	T	W	T	F	S
	☐	☐	☐	☐	☐	☐	☐
	☐	☐	☐	☐	☐	☐	☐
	☐	☐	☐	☐	☐	☐	☐
	☐	☐	☐	☐	☐	☐	☐
	☐	☐	☐	☐	☐	☐	☐
	☐	☐	☐	☐	☐	☐	☐
	☐	☐	☐	☐	☐	☐	☐
	☐	☐	☐	☐	☐	☐	☐
	☐	☐	☐	☐	☐	☐	☐

Notes

Reminders

Printed in Great Britain
by Amazon

46233049R10069